MONUMENTAL MOMENTS
IN AFRICAN AMERICAN HISTORY
By the President of the United States of America.
BLACK HERITAGE
CELEBRATING CULTURE!
BY CAROLE MARSH

Enslaved People Fight Back!

Nat Turner led an uprising of enslaved people in Virginia in 1831. His parents had been enslaved and forced to come to America. Nat believed that he was chosen to lead a fight against slavery.

Nat planned to attack slave owners and their families. He and about 75 other enslaved people set out on their campaign after midnight on August 21. They killed at least 57 people over two days.

Nat was captured six weeks after the uprising and hanged. Nat Turner's rebellion was one of several in which enslaved people fought against the system that enslaved them. Enslavers feared such rebellions and took harsh actions to prevent them.

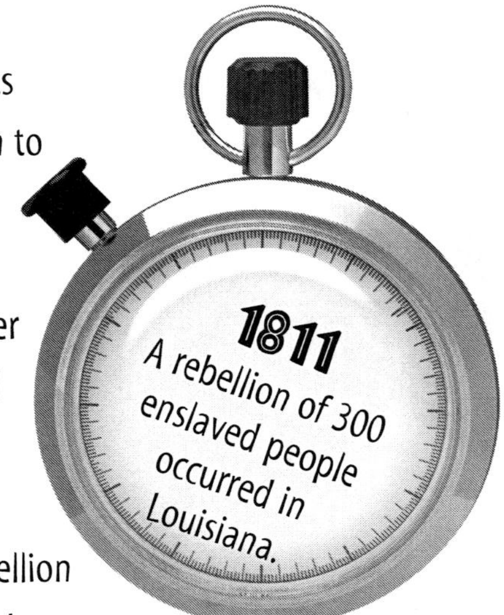

ACTIVITY

True or False?

1. ____ Nat was captured six weeks after the uprising.
2. ____ Massachusetts was the site of Nat Turner's Rebellion.
3. ____ Nat Turner and his men never killed anyone.
4. ____ Enslavers feared rebellions like Nat Turner's.
5. ____ Nat Turner was sent to prison for his role in the rebellion.

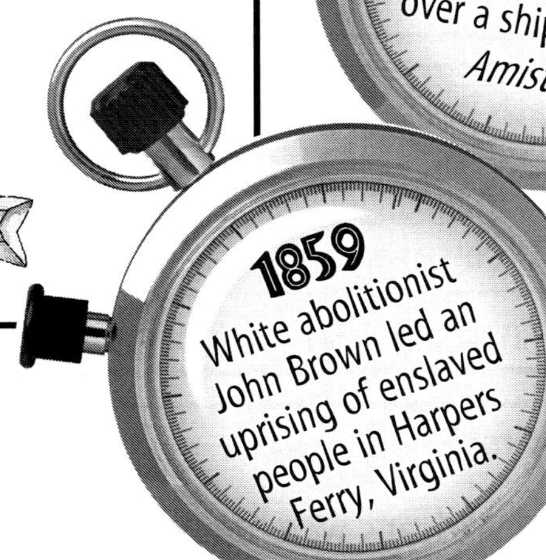

The Cotton Gin Changes History

In 1793, a man named Eli Whitney invented a machine that made a big impact on American history. Eli invented the cotton gin on a Georgia plantation. The cotton gin was a machine that took the seeds out of cotton. Before the cotton gin, enslaved people had to pull the seeds out of cotton by hand. That took a very long time.

A person operating a cotton gin could clean 50 times more cotton in a day than someone pulling the seeds out by hand. Planters realized they could produce much more cotton now that they had the cotton gin. So, they planted more cotton, and enslaved more people to grow and harvest it.

Slavery grew by leaps and bounds after the cotton gin was invented. Many more enslaved people were forced to work in the South where cotton was grown.

ACTIVITY

Circle the conditions that might explain why cotton was grown in the South.

warm weather	rocky soil	lots of rain
cold weather	lots of snow	good soil

ACTIVITY

Match the cause to its effect.

1. ____ Cotton seeds removed by hand
2. ____ Eli Whitney invents cotton gin
3. ____ Planters grow more cotton

a. more people enslaved to plant and harvest
b. people can clean cotton faster
c. takes a long time to clean cotton

Taking the Underground Railroad

Enslaved people longed to escape to freedom. And some of them did! Thousands of enslaved people traveled along the "Underground Railroad." This was not a railroad at all, but a network of helpful people and safe places where people fleeing slavery could hide.

People fleeing slavery on the Underground Railroad had to be very careful. They moved at night, and hid during the day. They hid in houses, barns, and in the woods. They crossed rivers at night with only the moonlight to guide them. It was a risky business, but the reward was freedom!

The Underground Railroad used people known as "conductors" to help those fleeing slavery escape. One of the most famous conductors was Harriet Tubman. She had escaped from slavery earlier in her life. She traveled to the South more than a dozen times and helped more than 100 people make it to freedom! She was a dedicated abolitionist (someone who is against slavery).

ACTIVITIES

Solve the code to find out what Harriet Tubman was called.

A	B	C	D	E	F	G	H	I	J	K	L	M	N	O	P	Q	R	S	T	U	V	W	X	Y	Z
✸	❁	✣	♣	➸	❤	❢	✲	✂	✆	☛	✈	✉	✿	☆	✦	✡	✎	❦	☎	➻	✚	✖	✍	✠	✓

__ __ __ __ __   __ __   __ __ __   __ __ __ __ __ __

✉ ☆ ❦ ➸ ❦   ☆ ❤   ✲ ➸ ✎   ✦ ➸ ☆ ✦ ✈ ➸

Harriet had some tricks up her sleeve to keep from being discovered. She headed south if she saw slave hunters. Why did she do that?

____

____

Harriet also carried a drug to quiet crying babies. Why did she do that? ____________

____

____

1852

A Book Changes Attitudes About Slavery!

In 1852, a novel made a tremendous impact on the anti-slavery movement in America. *Uncle Tom's Cabin* told a story about the terrible treatment of enslaved people by a cruel slave owner. People in the North were shocked by the story. It turned many people against slavery. The book became extremely popular and was made into a play.

Uncle Tom's Cabin was written by a woman named Harriet Beecher Stowe. She based the book on memories of living in Cincinnati, Ohio for 18 years. Those vivid memories included people fleeing slavery from nearby Kentucky on the Underground Railroad.

Harriet's book even got the attention of President Abraham Lincoln during the Civil War. He reportedly called Harriet "the little lady who made this big war."

ACTIVITIES

Write F for Fact, and O for Opinion

____ 1. *Uncle Tom's Cabin* was the best book ever written about slavery.

____ 2. Harriet Beecher Stowe lived in Cincinnati, Ohio.

____ 3. Abraham Lincoln did not like Harriet Beecher Stowe.

____ 4. Enslaved people were treated badly in *Uncle Tom's Cabin*.

____ 5. *Uncle Tom's Cabin* was made into a play.

____ 6. *Uncle Tom's Cabin* turned many people against slavery.

***Uncle Tom's Cabin* was translated into many languages. Solve the math problem to find out how many.**

6 + 4 + 2 – 6 + 8 + 6 – 1 + 1 = __________

People Returned to Slavery

Enslaved people trying to regain their freedom ran into many roadblocks. The Fugitive Slave Act of 1850 struck terror into the hearts of many people who had escaped to the North. The Fugitive Slave Act said that people who had fled slavery could be captured in any state and returned to their enslavers. This meant that people who had made it to freedom in the North were not safe. Even those who had been free for years could be returned! This law made many Northerners very angry.

A Supreme Court decision in 1857 took more rights away from enslaved people. Dred Scott was enslaved. His enslaver was in the U.S. Army. He took Dred Scott from the slave state of Missouri to the free state of Illinois. Then he went to the free territory of Wisconsin.

Dred Scott had to go back to Missouri with his enslaver, who died not long after settling there. Dred went to court to ask for his freedom. He said he should be free because he lived on free soil for a long time. The Supreme Court said no. They said an enslaved person was not a U.S. citizen. If he was not a citizen, he had no rights. If he had no rights, he could not go to court with a problem. He must remain enslaved. Northerners became angry again!

ACTIVITY

Put the events below in the correct order.

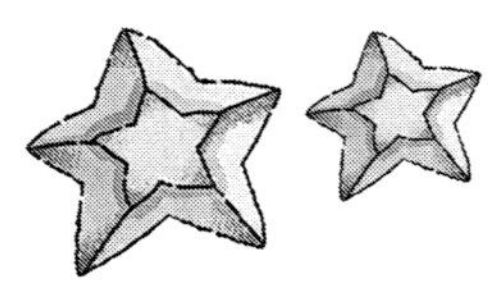

____ The Fugitive Slave Act was passed.

____ Dred Scott went back to Missouri after being in free territory.

____ Dred Scott's enslaver died.

____ The Supreme Court said that enslaved people were not U.S. citizens.

____ Dred Scott went to the free state of Illinois.

Did Dred Scott ever gain his freedom?

Yes! After the Supreme Court case, Dred and his wife were sold to old friends. They gave the Scotts their freedom!

Emancipation Proclamation Offers Freedom!

President Abraham Lincoln freed the enslaved people in the rebelling states during the Civil War! On September 22, 1862, he issued the Emancipation Proclamation. This document freed all enslaved people in areas held by the South. The focus of the Civil War shifted after the Emancipation Proclamation. After that, "freeing the enslaved people" became a goal for the Union Army.

Enslaved people held in Texas did not hear news of the Emancipation Proclamation until June 19, 1865. They found out when the Union Army landed in Galveston. "Juneteenth" is a holiday celebrating this event and the freeing of enslaved people.

ACTIVITY

Use the word bank to solve the Juneteenth crossword puzzle. You don't need clues. Just fit the words into the puzzle.

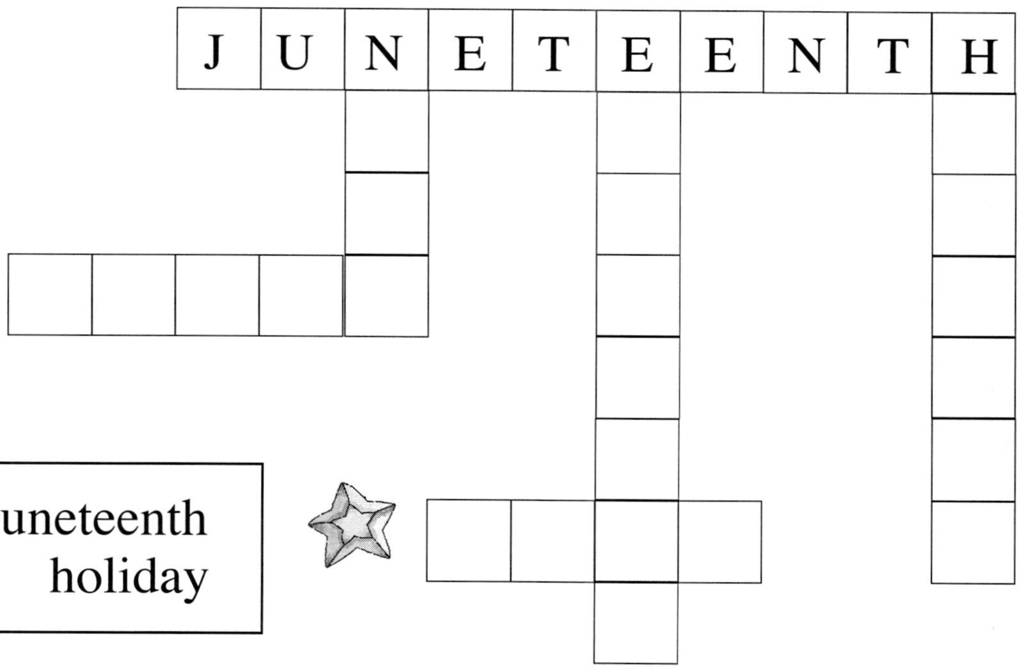

WORD BANK

free Texas Juneteenth
enslaved news holiday

New Amendments Protect Rights!

The Civil War ended in 1865. Enslaved people were free! The Union government knew that some changes needed to be made to protect the rights of people who had been enslaved. They decided to add three amendments to the U.S. Constitution.

These three amendments helped people who had been enslaved.

But it took a long time to change people's minds. Black people were denied their rights in many states.

The government passed the Civil Rights Act of 1866. It gave the government the power to punish those who denied Black people their rights.

ACTIVITY

Unscramble the words in the sentences below.

1. The 13th Amendment ________________ slavery.
   NDENBA
2. The 14th Amendment said that people born in the United States were ________________.
   ZICTINES
3. The 15th Amendment said that people could not be kept from voting just because they had been ________________.
   SEAELVDN

Black Colleges Provide Education!

After the Civil War, people who had been enslaved needed jobs. They needed places to get an education. Colleges were built to teach them.

One of the first Black colleges was called Howard University. It was named after General Oliver Howard. He was head of the Freedmen's Bureau. The Freedmen's Bureau helped people who had been enslaved get started in a new life. In 1867, he helped Howard University get started in Washington, D.C.

Another famous Black college was the Tuskegee Institute in Alabama. It opened in 1881. Students took regular subjects like math and science, but they learned other things, too. They learned practical things like farming, carpentry, brickmaking, and shoemaking.

ACTIVITY

Cross out every other letter starting with Y. You'll find out the name of the man in charge of the Tuskegee Institute when it opened.

Y B Z O R O X K V E M R

L T

P W S A F S R H P I C N D G A T G O H N

__ __ __ __ __ __   __

__ __ __ __ __ __ __ __ __ __

TRIVIA QUESTION

Look on the internet to find the answer to this question.

Are Howard University and the Tuskegee Institute still open today? Write your answer here.

ACTIVITY

Fill in the chart with information about Howard University and Tuskegee Institute.

College Name	Date Founded	Started By	Location	Still Open?
Tuskegee Institute				
Howard University				

Homer Plessy Challenges Segregation!

Black people continued to be discriminated against after the Civil War. Some states passed laws to keep Black people and white people separated. They had separate schools, restaurants, buses, and even bathrooms. This practice was known as "segregation."

A Black man named Homer Plessy ignored one of the laws. In 1892, he sat in the "whites only" section of a car on the Louisiana Railroad. Homer was put in jail. He took his case to court. He said he had a right to sit there. He said the 13th and 14th Amendments gave him that right. The case was known as *Plessy v. Ferguson.*

The judge said no. He said that Homer broke the law. This court decision said it was okay to have separate facilities for white people and Black people as long as they were equal.

ACTIVITY

Pull apart the sentence to learn the name of the segregation laws.

LawsthatseparatedBlackandwhitepeoplewereknownasJimCrowlaws.

____

ACTIVITY

Put these events in the correct order.

____ Homer Plessy sits in the "whites only" railroad car.

____ The Civil War ends.

____ Homer Plessy is found guilty of breaking the law.

National Groups Organize African Americans!

Segregation discriminated against African Americans. They were not treated equally. There was also violence against Black people. People formed organizations to fight against this unfairness.

The National Association for the Advancement of Colored People was formed in 1909. It was known as the NAACP, or "N–double A–C–P." It was started by both Black and white people. The NAACP became a very powerful organization. It fought for equal rights by going to court. The NAACP wanted to avoid violence.

Another group formed in 1910. It was known as the National Urban League. This group also wanted to help end segregation and discrimination. They also helped Black people with basic things they needed, such as jobs and houses.

Did You Know?
Both the NAACP and the National Urban League are still around today! They continue to work for the rights of African Americans.

What does it mean?

segregation:
forcing people of different races to live apart from each other

discrimination:
treating persons in an unkind or unfair way because they are different from you in some way

ACTIVITY

Fill in the blanks.

1. The NAACP was started by both Black and ________________ people. It fights for ________________ rights. The NAACP tries to avoid ________________________.
2. The National ______________ League was formed in ______________. This group helps people find ______________ and ________________.
3. ________________________ forces people of different races to live apart.
4. ________________________ treats people in an unkind or unfair way.

1864 TO 1943

George Washington Carver Helps Farmers!

George Washington Carver was a famous African American scientist. In fact, he was one of America's greatest scientists! He lived from 1864 to 1943.

George was a farming genius! He figured out how to create more than 300 products from the peanut. He also came up with many other products from soybeans, sweet potatoes, and pecans.

George was head of the agriculture department at Tuskegee Institute in Alabama. He told farmers to plant different crops each year to help put nutrients back into the soil. That suggestion helped farmers a lot. George Washington Carver's discoveries and ideas made the farming industry grow and grow in the South!

Other Black scientists and inventors include:

1791 Benjamin Banneker planned the layout of Washington, D.C. for George Washington.

1882 Jan Ernst Matzeliger invented a machine to make shoes.

1930s Charles Richard Drew developed the way to save blood plasma for blood transfusions.

ACTIVITY

Circle the qualities that describe Carver.

smart	sleepy
creative	curious

ACTIVITY

Circle the people that Carver helped during his career.

policemen	pilots
farmers	astronauts

Here are some other things that George Washington Carver made from plants ... bleach, marble, shaving cream, dye, talcum powder, shampoo, instant coffee, shoe polish, mayonnaise, buttermilk, ink, chili sauce, paper, sugar, rubber, and even steak sauce!

Harlem Renaissance Unleashes Black Culture!

Great creativity and new thoughts poured out of New York City between 1919 and 1937. This time period was known as the "Harlem Renaissance." Harlem is a part of New York City.

During this time, Black artists celebrated their pride and love for their roots and heritage. Talented African American writers produced books, plays, and poetry. Black musicians created jazz and blues music. Black artists became more popular than ever before! The Harlem Renaissance was a turning point for Black culture in America.

ACTIVITIES

Using the word HARLEM, write a word or phrase that describes the Harlem Renaissance.

H ______________________________

A ______________________________

R ______________________________

L ______________________________

E ______________________________

M ______________________________

Starting with Y, cross out every other letter to learn the name of the first African American to have his own television show.

Y N K A R T   W K B I X N T G   U C P O W L B E

__ __ __   __ __ __ __   __ __ __ __

Jesse Owens Wins Gold!

An African American athlete named Jesse Owens made a big impact in the 1930s. Jesse was very good in track-and-field events. In college, he broke three world records!

Jesse went to the 1936 Olympics in Berlin, Germany with the U.S. Olympic team. He won four gold medals! This upset Adolf Hitler, who was the leader of Germany at that time. He did not like Jesse because he was African American. Hitler believed that no race was as good as the German race. Jesse inspired Americans through his athletic skill and his victory in the face of a brutal dictator.

ACTIVITY

Put an F by the facts, and O by the opinions.

____ 1. Jesse Owens was African American.

____ 2. Jesse was on the 1936 U.S. Olympic team.

____ 3. The food in Germany is the best in the world.

____ 4. Jesse Owens is the world's best athlete.

____ 5. Jesse Owens inspired other athletes.

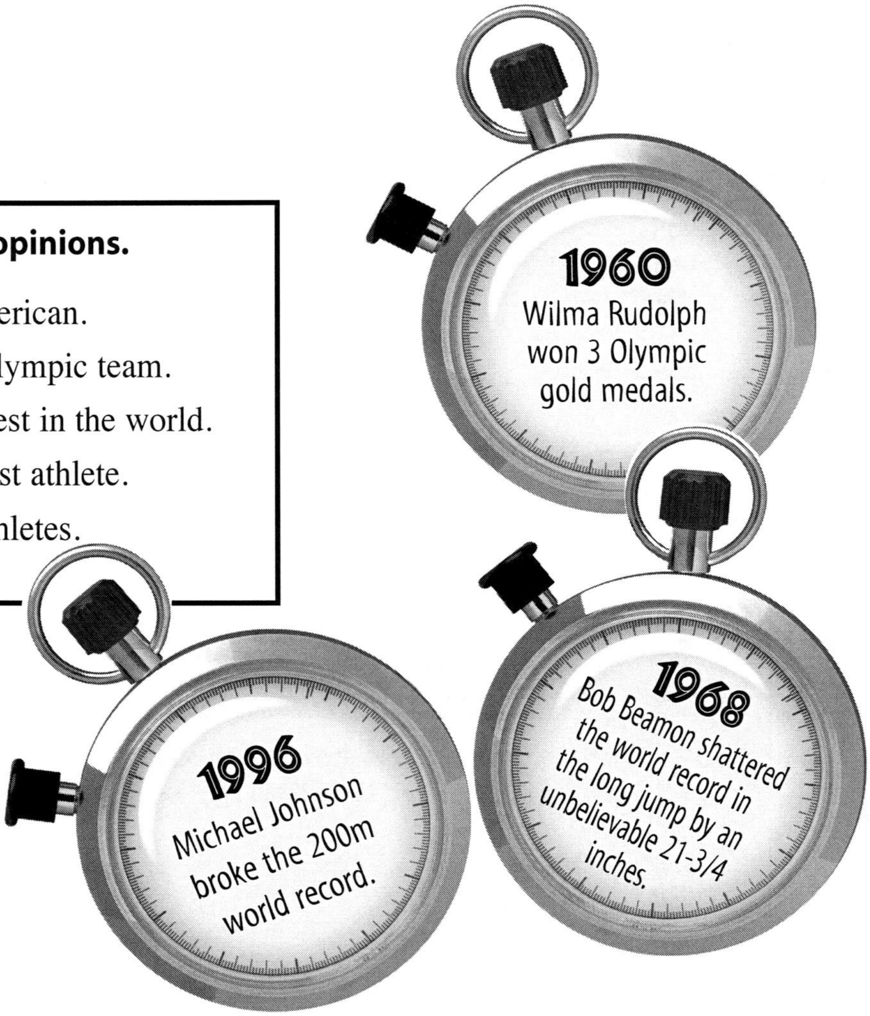

Jesse Owens inspired many other Black track-and-field athletes!

Jackie Robinson Plays Ball!

In 1947, Jackie Robinson became the first African American to play major league baseball. He played for the Brooklyn Dodgers. Some people did not think Black players should be allowed in the Major Leagues. Players threatened him, spat on him, and hit him with "wild" pitches. People in the stands yelled at him and sent him death threats.

Jackie was tough and played hard. He was named Rookie of the Year in 1947. That means he was the best new player in baseball. He was the National League's most valuable player in 1949. Jackie overcame incredible pressure. His courage and actions helped bring about opportunities for all African Americans in sports and other areas.

Jackie Robinson opened the door for many African American athletes!

ACTIVITY

List five words that describe Jackie Robinson.

____

____

____

____

____

ACTIVITY

Write the name of YOUR favorite athlete playing a sport today.

____

What sport does that person play?

____

Black Americans Serve Their Country!

African American soldiers fought in the Civil War. They fought in all-Black units. The first Black unit was the 54th Massachusetts Colored Regiment. By the end of the war, 186,000 Black soldiers had joined the Union Army. Black soldiers protested because they did not receive as much pay as white soldiers. Congress passed a law to make pay equal in 1864.

After the Civil War, two African American infantry units were formed. They fought cattle thieves, bandits, and Mexicans. They also fought in the Indian Wars in the late 1800s. The American Indians called these men "Buffalo Soldiers."

The Tuskegee Airmen were African Americans who served during World War II. They went through very hard training in Tuskegee, Alabama. Tuskegee Airmen were pilots, navigators, or bombardiers. Others worked in support jobs on the ground. The Tuskegee Airmen flew next to bombers traveling to Europe to protect them. Not one of their bombers was shot down!

WORD DEFINITION

bombardier: the person who releases the plane's bombs on the target

ACTIVITY

What's the Truth?
Write T for True and F for False.

____ 1. African Americans did not fight in the Civil War.

____ 2. Buffalo soldiers fought in the Indian Wars.

____ 3. Alabama was the state where the Tuskegee Airmen were trained.

____ 4. Tuskegee Airmen fought during World War II.

____ 5. Many bombers were shot down while being escorted by the Tuskegee Airmen.

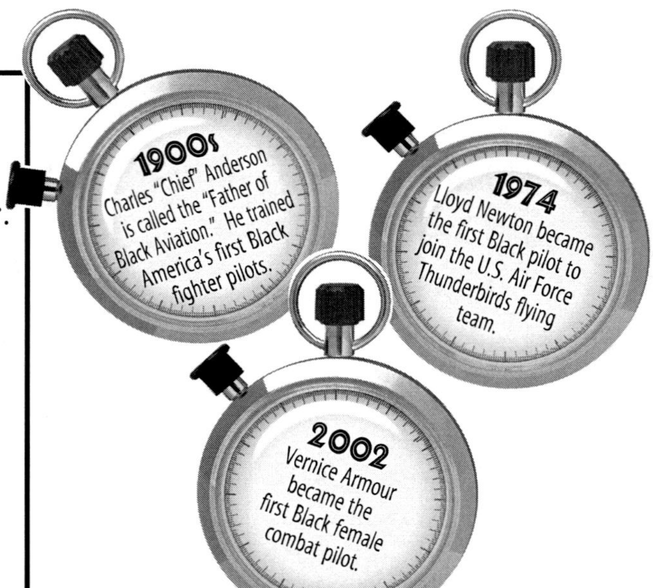

Supreme Court Brings Schools Together!

Until the 1950s, many states continued segregation. There were separate restaurants, movie theaters, and even drinking fountains! Schools were also separated. But things changed in 1954!

In Kansas, an African American third-grader named Linda Brown had to walk one mile to get to her Black elementary school. There was a white school a lot closer to her home. Her father asked if she could go there. The principal said no.

The case went to the U.S. Supreme Court. It was called *Brown v. Board of Education*. Linda's lawyer said that having separate schools was against the 14th Amendment. The Supreme Court agreed! They ruled that students should not be separated any longer!

WORD DEFINITION

integration: opening a school or other public place to people of all races

desegregation: stopping the practice of separating people of different races

ACTIVITY

Use the code below to find out the name of Linda Brown's lawyer. He later became a Supreme Court justice

❁	❄	❇	●	■	▲	◆	❖	♣	✧	★	✱	✺
A	B	C	D	E	F	G	H	I	J	K	L	M

➻	✓	✖	✚	✐	⇨	⑦	❂	✪	✯	★	✷	❍
N	O	P	Q	R	S	T	U	V	W	X	Y	Z

⑦ ❖ ❂ ✐ ◆ ✓ ✓ ● ✺ ❁ ✐ ⇨ ❖ ❁ ✱ ✱

_ _ _ _ _ _ _ _ _ _ _ _ _ _ _ _

Bus Boycott!

In the 1950s, many people rode buses to get to work. Rosa Parks was an African American woman in Montgomery, Alabama. After a long day at work, she took a seat in the Black section of a bus. A white man expected her to give up her seat when the "whites only" section filled up. Rosa refused, and she was arrested.

A man named Martin Luther King, Jr. led a protest against what happened to Rosa. He urged Black people to boycott the buses. This Montgomery Bus Boycott lasted for about a year. It cost the bus company a lot of money. The boycott ended when the U.S. Supreme Court ruled that the buses needed to be integrated.

WORD DEFINITION

boycott: to stop buying or using as a means of protest

Who Was Martin Luther King, Jr?

Dr. Martin Luther King Jr. was a Black minister who worked hard for equal rights. He told people to protest unfair laws without getting violent. He was one of the most important men in the history of the United States!

ACTIVITY

Unscramble the words in the sentence below.

____________ (A R S O) Parks was arrested. She refused to give up her ____________ (E S T A)

on a ____________ (U S B) to a ____________ (T I W H E) man. Later, the U.S. Supreme

____________ (O U C R T) ruled that buses needed to be ____________ (R N T G A I E T E D).

Sitting Down to Gain Rights!

African Americans used many peaceful ways to protest segregation. In 1960, they began "sit-in" protests. Four college students in North Carolina sat down at a lunch counter in a Woolworth's store. They were told they would not be served because they were Black. They refused to leave. The next day, they came back with more friends. They were not served again. Other college students heard about the "sit-in" and did the same thing in their towns.

In 1961, African Americans organized Freedom Rides. Black and white protesters rode on buses that drove throughout the South. The protesters wanted to draw attention to their fight for equal rights.

Some people in the South were angry about the Freedom Rides. They attacked the buses. The federal government stepped in to uphold the law and protect the Freedom Riders!

ACTIVITY

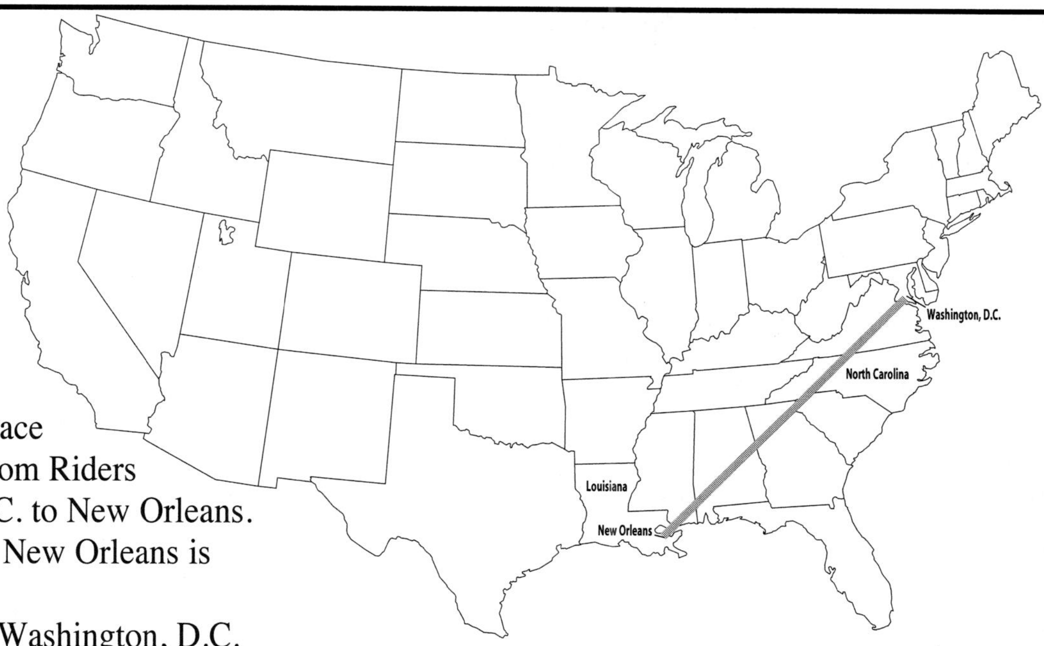

1. Use a red crayon to trace the route of the Freedom Riders from Washington, D.C. to New Orleans.
2. Color the state where New Orleans is located blue.
3. Draw a green star on Washington, D.C.
4. Find the state where the first sit-ins took place. Color it yellow.
5. Use a brown crayon to draw a circle around "the South."

March on Washington Makes History!

The fight for equal rights arrived in Washington, D.C. in 1963. People just poured into the city. More than 250,000 people traveled there! What was the reason? To tell Congress to vote YES on a law to give African Americans equal rights.

Dr. Martin Luther King, Jr. made a famous speech at the gathering. It is known as the "I Have a Dream" speech. He spoke on the steps of the Lincoln Memorial. King said that he dreamed of a world where Black and white children could play together in peace. The march made a big impact on America! The crowd was huge, but there was no violence. Dr. King always called for peaceful protest.

"I have a dream that my four little children will one day live in a nation where they will not be judged by the color of their skin but by the content of their character."
— Martin Luther King, Jr.

ACTIVITIES

Read the words of Dr. King's speech and fill in the blanks below.

Dr. King wanted his young children to live in a ______________

where the color of their ______________ did not matter as much as

the kind of ________________ they were.

Beginning with Y, cross out every other letter. You will learn the city and state where Martin Luther King, Jr. was born.

Y A B T P L K A W N F T P A   C G L E T O Q R Z G Z I H A

___ ___ ___ ___ ___ ___ ___,   ___ ___ ___ ___ ___ ___ ___ ___

Laws Guarantee Equal Rights!

- **Civil Rights Act**

This act said it was against the law to stop Black people from going to any public place they wanted. It also said the government would not give money to segregated schools. The act protected equal opportunities to get jobs for people of all races.

- **Voting Rights Act**

The 15th Amendment gave Black men the right to vote, and the 19th Amendment gave all women, including Black women, the right to vote. But many states said you couldn't vote if you couldn't read. Many poor Black people could not read, so they could not vote. The Voting Rights Act put a stop to that by banning all reading tests!

- **Equal Employment Opportunity Act**

This act forbade discrimination in government jobs because of race, color, religion, sex, or home country.

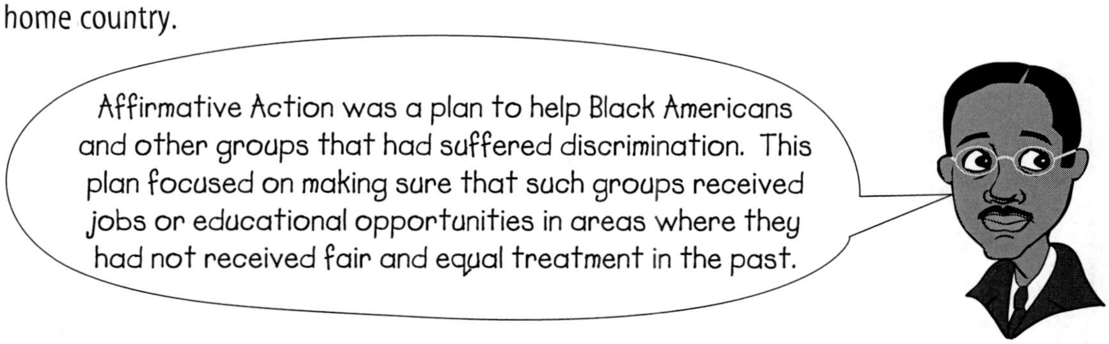

ACTIVITIES

Match the law with the result.

____	Civil Rights Act	A.	Forbade discrimination in government jobs
____	Voting Rights Act	B.	Banned reading tests
____	Equal Employment Opportunity Act	C.	African Americans could go to any public place

Talented People Set "Firsts" in Government!

Several African Americans blazed a new trail in government!

Thurgood Marshall became the first Black Supreme Court Justice in 1967. He was also a very smart civil rights lawyer. Thurgood won many cases that changed the lives of Black people, women, and the poor.

In 1968, Shirley Chisholm became the first African American woman elected to the U.S. Congress. She was also the first to run for president! She opened doors for many other women who wanted a career in politics. Many other African American women have served in Congress, thanks to Shirley's leadership.

ACTIVITIES

Write T for True and F for False.

1. ____ Thurgood Marshall was the first Black Supreme Court Justice.
2. ____ Marshall never worked on cases that affected African Americans.
3. ____ Shirley Chisholm was a U.S. Congresswoman.
4. ____ Shirley Chisholm ran for president.

Pull apart the words in the sentence below to find out one way that Shirley helped women.

Shirleyhiredallfemalesforherstaffwhenshejoinedcongress.

____

____

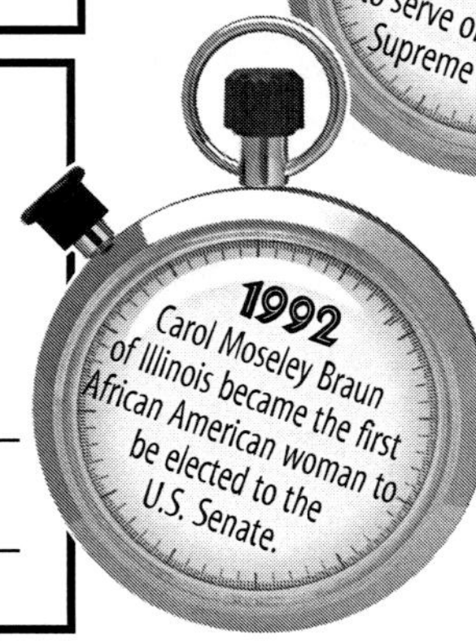

Black Astronauts Blast into Outer Space!

Two African Americans achieved "firsts" in outer space!

Guion Bluford was the first African American in space! His nickname is Guy. He started out as an Air Force pilot. Guy flew 144 combat missions in the Vietnam War. He became an astronaut in 1979. He flew on board the space shuttle *Challenger* in 1983. Guy flew on three more shuttle missions.

Dr. Mae Jemison was the first African American woman in space! Mae was a very bright student. She went to college when she was just 16 years old! She became a doctor, and worked with the Peace Corps in West Africa. Mae flew on board the space shuttle *Endeavour* in 1992.

ACTIVITIES

Mae Jemison speaks three other languages besides English. See if you can unscramble the languages below.

S N R S U I A ______________________________
Hint: It's really cold here; people like to wear fur hats.

P N J E A E A S ______________________________
Hint: People here like to eat raw fish.

H I W L S I A ______________________________
Hint: This is a language in Africa.

Solve the math problem to learn how many people applied to become an astronaut the year Guy Bluford was chosen for astronaut training.

5,000 + 1,000 + 6,000 + 100 – 2,000 – 100 = ______________________________

African Americans Serve the President!

Colin Powell and Condoleezza Rice are two important U.S. government leaders. They both served on the cabinet of President George W. Bush.

In 2001, Colin Powell became the first African American named U.S. Secretary of State. He was also a four-star general in the U.S. Army. He helped lead our country during the Persian Gulf War.

Condoleezza Rice served as the National Security Advisor to the president beginning in 2001. Her nickname is Condi. She was the first female and the first African American to serve in that role. In 2005, she became the first African American woman to become Secretary of State. In 2004 and 2005, a famous magazine named *Forbes* named her the world's most powerful woman!

ACTIVITY

M	C	Y	Y	K	S	Q	U	M	V	U	F	Q	L	L
X	O	D	R	M	E	A	S	F	U	W	N	L	H	M
C	N	U	R	A	R	Y	H	B	S	R	E	X	W	K
B	D	H	G	S	T	A	B	W	E	W	M	N	J	J
F	I	C	Q	N	O	E	R	E	O	P	Y	N	A	F
W	V	I	O	S	F	M	R	P	M	D	T	V	U	N
F	E	M	A	L	E	D	M	C	R	R	M	E	N	F
F	K	A	M	G	I	T	R	T	E	O	D	P	U	I
S	E	N	F	D	V	N	E	Q	V	S	Z	D	X	Z
B	Q	O	X	U	A	V	B	S	G	I	F	A	Z	N
J	T	H	H	I	K	E	K	T	W	V	P	R	S	D
T	N	E	M	N	R	E	V	O	G	D	Q	B	J	M
E	C	I	R	J	M	K	T	Q	V	A	U	K	Y	Q
F	F	Y	X	Y	N	V	C	A	W	S	H	K	K	Y
R	R	O	W	X	F	H	Y	H	H	I	N	T	O	T

Word Bank

COLIN
POWELL
GOVERNMENT
BUSH
RICE
CONDI
ARMY
SECRETARY
ADVISOR
FEMALE

Circle the words listed here in the word bank.

First African American President and Vice President!

2008 was a historic year for African American achievement! Barack Obama was elected 44th President of the United States, becoming the first African American to hold that office.

Barack Obama was a U.S. senator from Illinois before being elected U.S. president. In his victory speech on election night, he proclaimed that "change has come to America." In 2012, he was reelected for a second term.

In 2020, Kamala Harris also made history! She was elected the first female, Black, and Asian Vice President of the United States. She serves as vice president alongside President Joe Biden. Kamala was a U.S. senator from California before becoming vice president.

ACTIVITY

Make your own stamp! Design a postage stamp commemorating Barack Obama's election in 2008 as the first African American President of the United States.

More "Firsts" in African American History!

1773 Phillis Wheatley, an enslaved woman, writes *Poems on Various Subjects, Religious and Moral*, one of the first two books of verse by an American woman.

1827 John B. Russwurm, with Samuel E. Cornish, founds the nation's first Black newspaper, *Freedom's Journal*, in New York City.

1848 William Leidesdorff becomes the first African American millionaire when gold is found on his California property.

1853 Mary Ann Shadd Cary becomes the first African American woman to edit a newspaper.

1859 Harriet E. Adams Wilson is the first Black woman to publish a novel.

1869 Joseph H. Rainey becomes first Black man elected to the U.S. House of Representatives.

1870 Hiram R. Revels becomes first Black U.S. senator.

1907 Alain Leroy Locke becomes the first African American Rhodes scholar.

Early **1900s** Madame C.J. Walker becomes the first female African American millionaire. She invented the "Walker Method" treatment to straighten hair.

1950 Gwendolyn Brooks is the first African American to win a Pulitzer Prize for her book of poetry, *Annie Allen*.

1950 Earl Francis Lloyd becomes first African American to play in a National Basketball Association (NBA) game.

1951 Althea Gibson is first African American woman to play at the Wimbledon Tennis Tournament in England.

More "Firsts" in African American History!

1960 Six-year-old Ruby Bridges becomes the first Black child to desegregate a white school in New Orleans.

1959 Lorraine Hansberry's award-winning play, "A Raisin in the Sun," is the first play written by an African American woman to be produced on Broadway.

1964 Sidney Poitier is the first African American to win the Oscar for Best Actor for his work in "Lilies of the Field."

1965 Dr. Robert C. Weaver becomes first African American member of the U.S. Cabinet. He served as Secretary, Department of Housing and Urban Development.

1967 Charlie Sifford is the first African American to win a Professional Golfers' Association (PGA) event.

1975 Wally "Famous" Amos becomes the first African American to open a cookie retail business.

1975 General Daniel James, Jr. becomes the first African American four-star general.

1983 Alice Walker becomes the first African American to win the Pulitzer Prize in fiction for her novel, *The Color Purple*.

1993 Halle Berry becomes the first African American to win Best Actress.

2000 Robert Johnson, founder of Black Entertainment Television, becomes the first African American billionaire.

2001 Shirley Franklin is elected mayor of Atlanta, Georgia, and becomes first female African American mayor of a major Southern city.

2009 Eric Holder becomes first African American Attorney General of the United States.

2013 Jeh Johnson becomes the first African American Secretary of Homeland Security.

2015 Loretta Lynch becomes first female African American Attorney General of the United States.

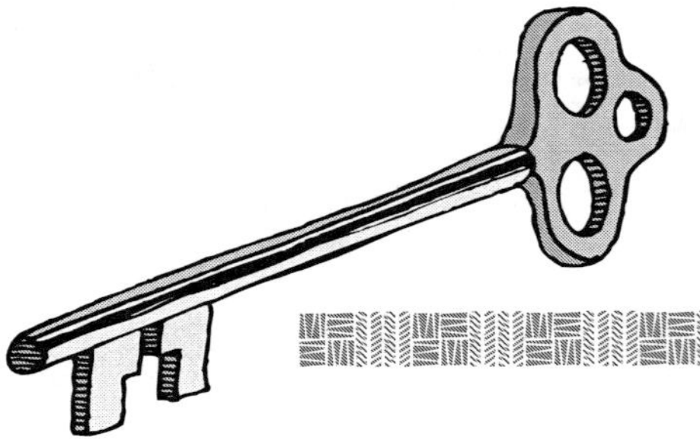

Answer Key!

Page 5
1. English pirates
2. 1,000
3. Enslaved Africans were stolen off a ship.

Page 6
1.T; 2.F; 3.F; 4.T; 5.F

Page 7
1. warm weather, lots of rain, good soil
2. 1.c; 2.b; 3.a

Page 8
1. Moses of her people
2. 1.To trick the slave hunters who would think she would only travel north.
   2.To keep babies quiet so she wasn't found by slave hunters.

Page 9
1. 1.O; 2.F; 3.O; 4.F; 5.F; 6.F
2. 20

Page 10
1, 3, 4, 5, 2

Page 11

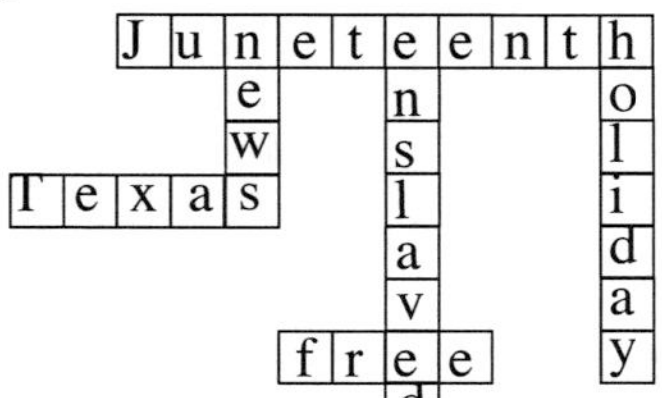

Page 12
1.forbid; 2.citizens; 3.enslaved

Page 13
1. Booker T Washington
2. Tuskegee Institute: 1888; Booker T. Washington; Alabama; Yes
   Howard University: 1867; Oliver Howard; Washington, D.C.; Yes

Page 14
1. Laws that separated Black and white people were known as Jim Crow laws.
2. 2, 1, 3

Page 15
1. white; equal; violence
2. Urban; 1910; jobs; houses
3. Segregation
4. Discrimination

Page 16
1. smart; creative; curious
2. farmers

Page 17
1. Answers will vary
2. Nat King Cole

Page 18
1.F; 2.F; 3.O; 4.O; 5.F

Page 19
1. Answers will vary
2. Answers will vary

Page 20
1.F; 2.T; 3.T; 4.T; 5.F

Page 21
Thurgood Marshall

Page 22
Rosa; seat; bus; white; Court; integrated

Page 23
1. students to trace line already on map;
2. Louisiana
3. students locate Washington, D.C.;
4. students locate North Carolina;
5. students circle southern region of U.S.

Page 24
1. nation; skin; person
2. Atlanta, Georgia

Page 25
C, B, A

Page 26
1. 1.T; 2.F; 3.T; 4.T
2. Shirley hired all females for her staff when she joined Congress.

Page 27
1. Russian; Japanese; Swahili
2. 10,000

Page 28